My Pet Worm

Written by Sally Morgan

Photographed by

Collins

Worms are long.

Some are thin. Some are thick.

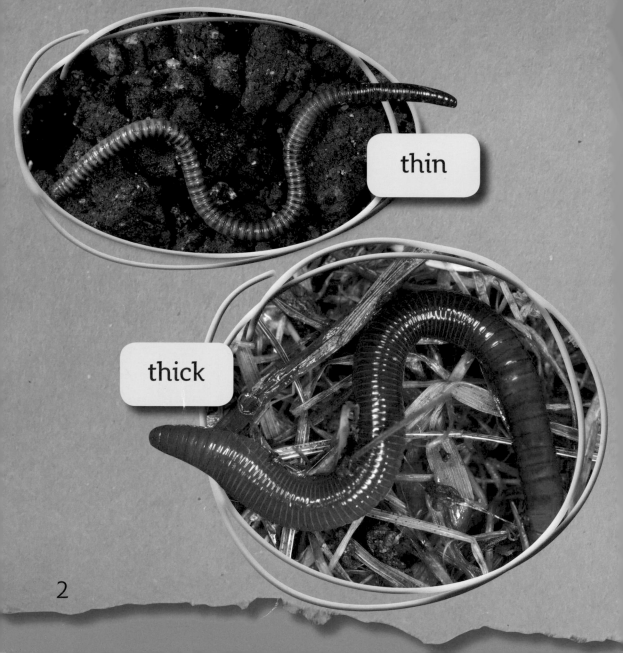

thin

thick

Worms live underground.

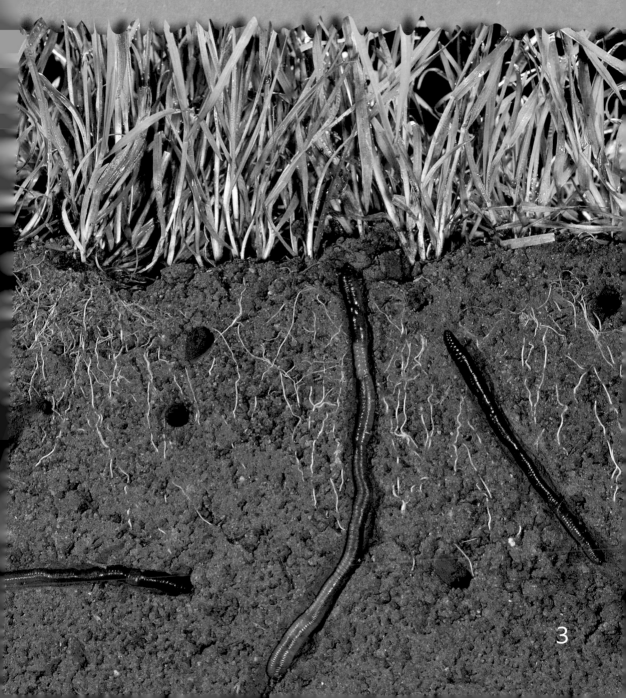

You can keep worms as pets.
Put some soil in a bottle.

Now, water the soil.

Find some worms.

Dig up some worms.

Put the worms in the bottle.

Find some food for them.

Keep your worms in a cool, dark place.

Check them and feed them every day.

Keep the soil damp.

Then, put your worms back outside.

Keeping a pet worm

Ideas for reading

Written by Clare Dowdall, PhD
Lecturer and Primary Literacy Consultant

Learning objectives: identify the constituent parts of two-syllable and three-syllable words to support the application of phonic knowledge and skills; apply phonic knowledge and skills as the prime approach to reading unfamiliar words that are not completely decodable; find specific information in simple texts; take turns to speak, listen to others' suggestions and talk about what they are going to do

Curriculum links: Science

High frequency words: how, live, out, water, back, home

Interest words: worm, long, thin, thick, underground, soil, cool, dark, damp, outside

Resources: whiteboard, plastic bottle, trowel, soil, worms, old tights and rubber band for cover, pens, paper

Word count: 73

Getting started

- Ask children to talk about their experiences of finding worms. Support them to take turns and listen to each other.

- Look at the front cover and read the title. Ask children to use the picture to predict what information the book will contain. Ensure children know how to read the *o* sound in the word *worm*.

- Model reading the blurb aloud fluently and ask children how they think we can keep worms as pets.

Reading and responding

- Turn to p2. Read the text aloud together. Look at the pictures of the worms and discuss what the children can see, ensuring they read and understand the labels.

- Turn to p3. Read the text and stop at the word *underground*. Discuss how this long word can be approached, e.g. by using phonic strategies, by looking for chunks of meaning and syllables, by using contextual cues.